People Who Have Helped the World

HENRY DUNANT

by Pam Brown

Picture credits

Borel-Boissonnas, pp. 24 (all), 25 (all); Boissonnas, p. 7 (below); V. Bouverat, p. 7 (above); Bridgeman Art Library, p. 13; British Red Cross Society, pp. 43, 58 (below); Camera Press, p. 23; (c) Roger Durand, pp. 11, 20, 21; Films du Jeudi, Paris, p. 18; Björn Fjórtoft, p. 58 (above); Heeresgeschichtliches Museum, Vienna (permanent loan from the Austrian Credit-Institutes), p. 16; International Committee of the Red Cross, Geneva, p. 4 (Museo Nazionale del Risorgimento, Turin), pp. 29, 30, 32 (Kriegsarchiv, Vienna), 34 (both), 35 (top), 39, 41, 42 (below), 44 (both), 45 (all), 46 (both), 47, 48 (all), 50 (both), 51 (both), 52 (top left and right), 57 (left); League of Red Cross and Red Crescent Societies, Geneva, pp. 42 (above), 52 (below left), 53, 54, 56; Liliane de Toledo, pp. 55, 57 (right), 59 (both); Mansell Collection, pp. 12, 33, 35 (below), 36, 37; Musée du Vieux Genéve, p. 9; Soviet Red Cross, p. 49.

Cover painting by Borin van Loon; map drawn by Geoffrey Pleasance

Exley Publications would like to thank the International Committee of the Red Cross, the League of Red Cross and Red Crescent Societies, the Henry Dunant Society of Geneva, and the British Red Cross Society for their help in providing information. We would further like to thank the ICRC and the League for their most generous help in providing pictures and in checking the manuscript.

Our thanks also go to Mr. Roger Durand — historian, teacher, and President of the Henry Dunant Society of Geneva — for permission to consult the manuscript of his biography of Henry Dunant.

North American edition first published in 1989 by
Gareth Stevens, Inc.
7317 West Green Tree Road
Milwaukee, WI 53223 USA

First published in the United Kingdom in 1988 with an original text
© 1988 by Exley Publications Ltd.
Additional end matter © 1989 by Gareth Stevens, Inc.

Library of Congress Cataloging-in-Publication Data

Brown, Pam, 1928-
    Henry Dunant.

    (People who have helped the world)
    Includes index.
    Summary: Describes how a young Swiss businessman, accidentally viewing the bloody Battle of Solferino in 1859, was shocked at the lack of care given the wounded and went on to found the International Red Cross.
    1. Dunant, Henry, 1828-1910--Juvenile literature. 2. Philanthropists--Switzerland--Biography--Juvenile literature. 3. Red Cross--Biography--Juvenile literature. [1. Dunant, Henry, 1828-1910. 2. Philanthropists. 3. Red Cross. 4. Solferino, Battle of, 1859] I. Title. II. Series.
HV569.D8G75   1988   361.7'7   [B] [92]   88-4917
ISBN 1-55532-849-0
ISBN 1-55532-824-5 (lib. bdg.)

Series conceived and edited by Helen Exley
Research: Margaret Montgomery and Diana Briscoe
Series editor, U.S.: Rhoda Irene Sherwood
Editorial assistant, U.S.: Scott Enk
Additional end matter, U.S.: Ric Hawthorne

Printed in Hungary

HENRY DUNANT

Founder of the Red Cross,
the relief organization dedicated to helping
suffering people all over the world

by Pam Brown

Gareth Stevens Publishing
Milwaukee

The Battle of Solferino

It was growing dark. The wounded men were struggling to breathe hot, dusty air, calling for help in ever-weakening voices. Some had comrades crouched beside them, but there was little they could do to ease their suffering. They had no medical supplies, no food, no water. They could only grasp the hands of the dying and comfort them as best they could, hoping that a stretcher would come before it was too late.

Only a few hours before there had been only noise and movement — the crash of cannons, the thundering of gun carriages, the rattle of muskets, and the cries of men caught up in the madness of battle. Now all was desolation. A horse screamed in agony a little way off, and one of the troopers pulled himself to his feet.

"Won't be a minute, my old friend."

Pierre stumbled away, skirting the abandoned guns and the sprawled corpses of French and Austrian soldiers. After a while, the wounded man heard a shot and then silence, a silence broken only by droning flies and the groans of thirsty men.

Pierre came back.

"A little water. Please. There was a pond back there. I remember it."

Pierre shook his head: "It's full of dead men. There's nothing."

The resulting chaos

It was 1859 and the battleground was in Italy, at Solferino. In books about the attempts to unite the Italian states, Solferino is portrayed as a decisive victory. But it was bought at the cost of thousands of lives.

This was expected. After the hideous slaughter at an earlier battle, a famous general had said: "Omelettes are not made without breaking eggs." Soldiers could

On June 24, 1859, the armies of the Austrian Empire and the Franco-Sardinian Alliance fought a 16-hour battle near the northern Italian village of Solferino. It was a particularly bloody fight, with forty thousand men dead or wounded.

As with all major wars before, there was little medical aid for the wounded. But a passing businessman, Henry Dunant, volunteered to help. The suffering he saw changed his life and would change attitudes across the world.

5

be replaced. The chaos after a battle was seen as the natural, inevitable outcome of war.

There have been many battles since that hot June day at Solferino — battles fought with even more lethal weapons. Today, however, there are well-equipped ambulances, with doctors and nurses standing by to help.

And always visible, painted on the tents, huts, and vehicles, is the universal symbol of the Red Cross or the Red Crescent, indicating a place of refuge, protected from attack by international agreement. We see these signs so often that we take them for granted. Yet until Solferino, the idea of such a symbol did not exist.

There was a civilian at Solferino, a businessman who had gone to Italy simply to further his financial interests. What he saw at Solferino changed his life and the lives of millions. Out of his horror at the suffering of that battle was to grow the Red Cross and Red Crescent movement.

His name was Henry Dunant.

Early days

Jean Henri* Dunant was born in Geneva, Switzerland, a city beside a great shining lake and surrounded by mountains. It was early summer — the eighth of May, 1828. He was the first of five children of prosperous and respected parents. Even the house where he was born seemed to breathe respectability.

Henry grew up proud of his ancestry, for both his father and mother came from what were considered "good" families. They were people who were more concerned with the care of the community than with personal wealth.

The family was solidly respectable and his father, Jean-Jacques, took his duties as a Swiss citizen very seriously. One of his concerns as a volunteer member of the Office of Guardianships and Trusteeships was the welfare of young people and prisoners.

When Henry was about seven, the family went on a trip down the Rhone Valley to Marseilles in the south of France — a great adventure that introduced these landlocked Swiss children to the wonders of the sea.

Henry Dunant was born Henri Dunant, but later in life he chose to adopt the English spelling of Henry.

6

"I shall write a book"

But the journey was not all happiness. Mr. Dunant had agreed to visit Swiss criminals who were working out their sentences at the jail in Toulon. He took Henry with him.

Henry was a sensitive little boy, probably made more so by his gentle, pious Mama. To see these men taking exercise in the dark prison yard, the sky just a little blue tent above the drab stone walls, horrified him. Later he saw the prisoners on the roads, shackled and working at the soul-destroying job of breaking stones. To the well-fed and well-clothed boy, the haggard men seemed to be outcasts from society.

The small boy walked away in silence, then suddenly said to himself, "When I am big I shall write a book to save them."

He dreamed of these men chained, without hope or dignity, shut off from their families and every human joy. The memory haunted him for the rest of his life.

But soon the family returned to Geneva and, for the time being at least, the Toulon experience faded from Henry's life. It was a secure and happy life. Best of all were the visits to his grandparents' farm, where the children could run in the gardens. Long after he was grown, Henry could list the fruits that grew there, as though he could still taste their sweetness.

When he was ten, Henry went away to school. In later life he had little recollection of his lessons, only of the books he read while he nibbled the figs, raisins, nuts, and candied plums that a kindhearted uncle had sent to him at school!

In 1842, when Henry was fourteen, there were few signs of his future talents. In fact, he was asked to leave his school. He showed an early writing talent, but even that was demonstrated only by a detailed description of a plum cake or a blow-by-blow account of a meal on a visit to Marseilles!

At sixteen Henry was still very young for his years. It almost seemed that he was reluctant to grow up and leave the happy, secure world in which his mother reigned. All his life, part of him would yearn for the lost world of childhood.

Henry Dunant's birthplace in Geneva, Switzerland.
Below: Dunant adored his mother for her gentleness. She had a lifelong influence on him.

7

Dunant, the humanitarian

By eighteen, Dunant was a deeply devout, serious young man. His family had already left the official church and had joined the Church of the Awakening, a group that insisted on active charity. The more people had been given, the more they should give to others. One concept they believed in appealed strongly to Dunant. It was the idea of unity among all peoples, of cooperation, and of mutual respect.

He felt deeply for the poor and became a member of the League of Alms, whose members tried to bring spiritual and material help to the poor and sick of Geneva. Remembering the prisoners at Toulon, Dunant began to visit the city prison every Sunday afternoon. He read to the prisoners, opening up the world to these men who were shut away behind stone walls and iron bars. They recognized his enthusiasm and concern and looked forward to his visits.

Dunant and the YMCA

By the time he was twenty-one, Dunant had organized the young evangelists he knew into an active group that met every week at his home.

By 1853 he had started a career in banking, which his parents considered a very good job. He did well and worked hard in the banking business. He felt he had a religious duty to use his talents to succeed in business and then to use the success and talent to work for people in need. He became deeply involved in the establishment of the Young Men's Christian Association, the YMCA, which had been set up in London.

He was so enthusiastic that his fellow workers found him difficult to deal with at times. One friend wrote: "What a pity it is that he is so lacking in judgment. Otherwise he would be a jewel. He has amazing zeal and energy."

That same fire of enthusiasm was to be invaluable in Dunant's life, but his lack of practicality and discipline was to be costly to him.

In 1855, Henry Dunant's belief in cooperation between countries and among different branches of

the Protestant faith encouraged him to suggest that there should be a World Alliance of the Young Men's Christian Association. He proposed that the delegates should meet every year in each of the countries in turn. And so, in August 1855, the first of these world conferences was held in Paris, and Dunant was instrumental in helping the YMCA become the strong worldwide movement it is today. He was the main author of the YMCA charter used by all members today.

Dunant's sympathy for all people kept in subjection found a new object in slavery. In the United States, millions of blacks, whose African ancestors had been captured by force and with great cruelty, were the property of white people. When Dunant learned of this at this early age, he became a champion for the freedom of American slaves.

Dunant's dream was one of universal tolerance. His vision was clear, simple, and beautiful. And somehow, right from the start, he could awaken in other people enthusiasm for a cause that they could turn into practice — the effort to help the enslaved.

The Geneva of Henry Dunant's youth was a prosperous place if you were born into the elegant society of the wealthy. But there was also hardship, even starvation, amid the plenty. One of young Henry's earliest experiences was a visit with his father to a jail. He was appalled by what he saw: "I will write a book about it when I grow up," he vowed.

Algeria

Business demands now took Dunant to Algeria, in North Africa. He had never come into contact with the world of North Africa before, and he was enchanted. The Europeans of the nineteenth century were in love with what they saw as an exotic, romantic world. But they also believed in taking over other countries and empire building.

Dunant was very much a man of his time in this respect. A devout businessman, he saw opportunities for both spreading the Christian Gospel and making a great deal of money. He decided to set up a farm and a grain mill in Algeria and began to try to raise the money and support he needed for his new business.

He went back to Geneva to try to persuade investors to put up the capital for what he believed could be a more profitable business.

Dunant found the support he needed and built his mills. But his enthusiasm had blinded him to many difficulties. As the years went by, his business began to fail. An aunt died and left him money, which he fed into his mills, but success still evaded him. By now he was thirty years old. The core of the problem was that Algeria was a French colony. Because Henry Dunant was not French he had difficulty trying to obtain the concessions he needed for a second water source to drive the mills.

He came to believe that his only hope was to approach Emperor Napoleon III of France directly in an attempt to obtain the concessions he desperately needed. This would have been a difficult enough task if the Emperor had been in Paris — but he was not: he was fighting a war in Italy.

Napoleon III had announced, on May 3, 1859, that he was taking command of the French army in Italy. He wanted to release Italy from the domination of Austria and guarantee that there would be a friendly nation on the French frontier.

The campaign against Austria was successful from the start. The bayonet, the terrible weapon of Napoleon III's French foot soldiers, played a great part in the victories.

The Italians were fighting with Napoleon's help to

gain their freedom from the Austrians, and the decisive battle of the war was about to begin.

Dunant pursued Napoleon. Dressed in a white tropical suit, a boost to his self-confidence among the glittering army uniforms, he tracked the Emperor down just in time to arrive for the Battle of Solferino.

Solferino — the battle

The Austrians had marched all night to the allied position. They had intended to attack the allied forces of France and Italy at nine in the morning, but the Allies decided to catch them unawares. Long before dawn on June 24, 1859, the allied troops were roused from their sleep. They were not given food. In the summer dawn, with only a quick drink of black coffee, they advanced in the direction of the enemy.

The Austrians, who had only just settled after the forced march, were half asleep and had no time for food either. They went into battle on nothing but a double ration of alcohol. In the fifteen-hour battle that was to come, the men of both sides suffered not only from the effects of the brutal fighting but also from hunger, thirst, and exhaustion.

It was common in those days for civilian people to go up onto high ground and watch a battle as if it were an event staged for the theater. People would sometimes even take a picnic lunch and eat as they watched the killing from a safe distance. The battle looked almost like it was being fought by toy soldiers. But these were really 300 thousand men of flesh and blood facing each other.

The battle, known as the Battle of Solferino, raged in and around four villages situated in a straight line on the northern Italian heights near Solferino.

Dunant would later write: "The Austrians advanced in perfect formation along the beaten tracks. In the centre of the solid masses of Whitecoats, floated the Colours, yellow and black blazoned with the Imperial Eagle.... Against them moved the French Force, a dazzling spectacle in the brilliant Italian sun. There, the Guards could be seen, the gleaming ranks of Dragoons and Guides, Lancers and Cuirassiers."

Henry Dunant's mills in Algeria were to cause him a great deal of trouble. Henry was a passionate member of a radical Christian church, the Eglise du Reveil *(Church of the Awakening). This breakaway church insisted that its members had to give back to society if they had received more than others. Making money was to be applauded, but a true Christian commitment demanded more. Henry took lessons in Arabic and vowed that he would see that his Algerian workers were happy and well paid.*
(Photo © Roger Durand)

The Battle of Solferino in 1859, between the French with their allies and the Austrians, turned out to be one of the bloodiest battles of the nineteenth century. In one long day 300 thousand soldiers fought; forty thousand were wounded or died. "This was hand-to-hand fighting, indescribably hideous," wrote Dunant. "Austrian and allied troops trampled on one another over the bleeding corpses, felling their adversaries with rifle butts... it was butchery."

Blood and butchery

On the battlefield there was no illusion of pageantry or spectacle. The din of battle hammered at the ears — a din made up of the screams of wounded men and horses, the crash of cannon fire and the shriek of the Austrian bullets overhead. It was chaos. It was a confusion of dirt and smoke, of figures that fought, ran, and fell. Men fought with gun, bayonet, sword and, when all else was lost, with stones and bare hands. Desperate men, in the madness of battle, tore at the enemy with their teeth. Men fell under a hail of musket balls or the hoofs of maddened horses. Swords cut them down; cannon balls smashed them into the earth.

The soldiers fought through village after village along a twelve-mile front, leaving behind them, across the otherwise peaceful countryside, the horrors of death and destruction.

Dunant was horrified by the sheer insanity of the fighting. There was no mercy for the wounded. Battle-crazed men hammered to death those who had fallen, using the butts of their rifles.

There was not a drop of water. The sun scorched down on the exhausted men, but still they fought on.

After hours of combat, the Austrian stronghold at Solferino was broken, and the French guns on the hilltops began shelling the Austrian army.

The Austrians retreated in panic. The soldiers had lost all hope and fled.

The night after the battle

The retreating Austrians had gathered as many wounded as they could in any carts or carriages they could lay their hands on. But thousands of wounded and dying soldiers were left alone and afraid. They lay in pain on the blood-soaked battleground.

The light was fading.

All across the vast expanse of the abandoned battlefield, French soldiers wandered, but with a purpose. They were searching for their fallen comrades. But even when they found them, there was little these soldiers, inexperienced in medicine, could do to help.

Night fell and the hills were dotted with campfires. At least they had a little warmth, but there was no medical equipment, no food, no water. Many soldiers had been ordered to stack their knapsacks when they went into the attack. These had been lost or stolen by the local people. These poor people needed food, and many needed articles of clothing. They saw any such equipment left by the soldiers as a gift from heaven and took it without guilt.

The lack of water was the worst torment: what pools existed were darkened with blood. Men with some water in their drinking cans could not bear to keep it from their dying comrades, so they too were soon racked with thirst. They slept as best they could.

Napoleon III. Henry Dunant had followed him to Italy to plead for concessions for his business venture in Algeria. Instead, Dunant found himself pleading for medical assistance for thousands of wounded.

"The earth was soaked and running with blood."
Henry Dunant

13

The thousands of wounded

June 25 dawned on a nightmare landscape of ruined fields, broken and abandoned weapons, exhausted and desperate men — and the dead.

The total of Austrians, French, and Italians killed and wounded in the battle numbered 3 field marshals, 9 generals, 1,566 officers of all ranks, and 20,000 ordinary soldiers. Two months later these numbers doubled. Forty thousand men were killed or wounded on that dreadful day.

A night without shelter or water had killed many who might otherwise have survived, and those still alive were in a terrible condition. Thieves had invaded the battlefield by night and stolen all they could from the living as well as the dead.

The wounds were horrible, full of debris and dirt. In those days before antibiotics and antiseptics, many men were doomed to an agonizing death, however slight the initial injury.

Looking at the dead, Dunant could not get it out of his mind that only the day before these men had been alive. He looked down at one young soldier, "his fine manly face hardly recognizable, for sabre and shrapnel had caught him," and thought of all the care and love that had surrounded him in the past, only to have him end like this.

Death in war is as terrible now as it was then. But now soldiers carry emergency rations, packs of dressings, and drugs. A man's pain can be eased; infections can be prevented; the journey to a medical base can be made a little more bearable. At Solferino and other such battles, men were taken from the field of battle on primitive stretchers or slung across mule packsaddles. They were given nothing to lessen their agony.

There were field medical posts — of sorts. Although marked by black flags, in the heat of battle many were fired on. Even if they had been fired on, the help they could offer was primitive. The doctors knew little about preventing infection and less about painkillers. For a long time, doctors had relied on speed to lessen the shock of amputation. They prided themselves on the number of seconds they took to cut off an arm or a leg!

The wounded were taken from the Solferino battle-field to the nearby villages, where every church and convent had been turned into an emergency hospital. The barracks, the churches, even private houses, were packed with wounded men. Straw was put down on the streets and men lay there under awnings of sail-cloth to shield them a little from the Italian sun.

Dunant takes charge

Dunant could not stand idly by and went to help. Though he had worked with sick people before, he had no experience of anything remotely like this. Stupid-ity, ignorance, and superstition were adding to the tortures of thirst and agonizing injuries. Some men had been wearing filthy bandages for hours and were suffering torments as the bandages tightened over the swollen, rotting gashes.

Dunant started work in Castiglione, one of the villages that had been overrun in the battles. Over nine thousand wounded were brought to Castiglione alone. Dunant found water and bandages and moved along the rows of soldiers, doing whatever he could for them — moistening their parched lips and trying to clean their wounds. Often he could do nothing but comfort a dying man.

There were few women who could help. Most were caring for the wounded officers they had taken into their homes. But Dunant persisted. Water and food had to be gotten to the men. Their wounds had to be cleaned and their dressings changed.

He took a church called Chiesa Maggiore under his special care and used it as his headquarters. Five hundred soldiers lay inside, and a hundred just outside on the streets. From the Chiesa Maggiore he organized his growing band of helpers.

Dunant's "nurses," ordinary untrained women, followed him into the horror. They had no nursing experience, but they were kind and patient and gentle. They were Italians and the wounded were foreigners whom they feared. But Dunant kept repeating, "Tutti fratelli" — "They are all brothers." Soon the local people began saying it to each other too: "Tutti fratelli, tutti fratelli."

"There was water and food, but even so, men died of hunger and thirst; there [were] plenty of [bandages], but there were not enough hands to dress wounds; most of the army doctors had to go on to Cavriana, there was a shortage of medical orderlies, and at this critical time no help was to be had. Somehow or other a volunteer service had to be organized; but this was very difficult amid such disorder; what was worse, a kind of panic seized the people of Castiglione…."

Henry Dunant

A typical "ambulance" at Solferino. In fact there were no ambulances — any available vehicles were used to carry the wounded. They were uncomfortable and the bumpy journey hurt and killed many wounded men. If a cart like this was surrounded by soldiers in the thick of battle, there was no way the enemy could know that it was carrying the wounded, so it was liable to attack yet again. In less than ten years, Dunant would change all that.

Dunant rounded up little boys and organized them to run between the churches and the nearest fountains, to keep up the supply of fresh water. The boys worked for three days, some without rest.

Henry Dunant gave orders to soldiers, doctors, villagers, and volunteers. In the chaos, everyone obeyed. He insisted that two doctors taken as prisoners of war should be freed to help. He also insisted that doctors care for all the wounded regardless of nationality. He got his way.

Dunant was a businessman and a man experienced in organizing charity work. He put all his skills to this new use. His coachman went to a nearby farm and came back loaded down with useful supplies.

Dunant did all he could. He crouched beside the men and took down their last messages, promising to write to their parents, their wives, or their sweethearts. Often it seemed to lift a great weight from the men's minds — and they died quietly.

In the nearby towns and villages, hundreds of people were, like Henry Dunant, doing everything they could to help the wounded and dying men. Like him, they felt the total futility of it all. Like him, they could do nothing except work on and on and on.

"If only I had been looked after sooner"

The few doctors and the volunteers worked without sleep, but Dunant was appalled by the lack of organization. Courage and kindness were all very well, but surely these vast numbers of casualties could have been foreseen? Surely more carts, more bandages, more medicines, more helpers could have been ready to deal with them? Dunant thought of all the battles that had been fought in his own lifetime and of all those fought down the centuries. His mind reeled: so much suffering, and so much of it unnecessary.

An old sergeant who had fought through many campaigns in his life said to Dunant, suddenly and with great bitterness, "If I had been looked after sooner I might have lived, and now, by evening I shall be dead." Later Dunant wrote sadly, "And by evening he was dead."

Dunant's frustration, his indignation, and his sorrow were to lead to the founding of the Red Cross.

But that was in the future. He had no time now even to dream of such a possibility. He must do what he could to help those who needed him.

"They are all brothers"

The women were wonderful. The soldiers were all foreigners, all strangers, and yet the poor villagers cared for them with gentleness and patience and affection. "Tutti fratelli," they would say repeating Henry Dunant's words: "They are all brothers."

But as day followed terrible day, Dunant felt a great weariness bordering on despair eating into him. Whatever he did, it was never enough; however long he worked, there was always something else that desperately needed to be done. He dared not stop, feeling that if he did a man could be without water, another without anyone beside him when he died. Dunant worked without sleep for three days and nights, until the surviving men could begin to be moved to city hospitals.

It would eventually take three weeks to find and

"The Italian ladies who attended the wounded were amazed to see that their meat rations were simply laid on the blankets and had to be eaten with the fingers.... If soup was provided, if they wanted any, the wounded had to use the receptacles at the foot of their beds."

*John Bapst,
missionary and educator*

bury all those who had died at Solferino, because their bodies were scattered across the twelve-mile front of the battlefield.

The wounded are moved away

With the battle over, the wounded were packed into every available building in the surrounding villages. There were nine thousand wounded in the village of Castiglione, where Dunant was. Dunant, still dressed in his white suit, worked among the wounded and dying. By leadership and personal example, he organized a team of three hundred volunteers to help him. (Scene from the film of Dunant's story, The Man in White, *filmed in Chiesa Maggiore.)*

Many men who had survived those first days were now considered fit enough to be moved and were loaded into ambulance carts and ox wagons. Slowly they lurched away, the sun scorching down on them and great clouds of dust marking their progress.

At every halt along those bumpy roads, the local women came out of their houses. They were often very poor people who had lost their food to the army on the way to the battle. But now they gave the men fruit, soup, and wine, washed away the dust, and changed their bandages.

As soon as the situation in Castiglione seemed under control, Dunant went to Brescia, the town to which many of his patients had been moved. Fifteen thousand beds had been improvised. The villagers had

reacted to this invasion of sick soldiers with incredible hospitality. It was a town of forty thousand inhabitants, and at one point they were grappling with thirty thousand sick and wounded. The 140 who were doctors working with medical students and volunteers amazed Dunant by their dedication.

Dunant recognized many of his patients from Castiglione. They were better cared for now, but delay was taking its toll. Fever and gangrene were killing men that Dunant had hoped would recover.

Dunant's dream of a better way

All the time, Dunant kept thinking that things should be better than this. Surely there were people willing to help if only they were organized and understood what was needed. Later Dunant wrote, "All this kindness, all this good will, and still men die. In the face of so great an emergency what could be done by a handful of enthusiasts, all isolated and dispersed?"

As so often happens, Dunant would later write, "at the end of a week or ten days, the charitable zeal of the people of Brescia, sincere as it was, began to chill off. With a few honorable exceptions, the people grew tired and weary."

The situation was driving Dunant to despair. The supplies were there, the willing people were there — but there was no proper organization. Every single day, hundreds of men were still dying. Gradually the solution would crystallize: competent trained volunteers, sent by societies approved by the authorities, could easily overcome all these difficulties. Today it seems obvious, but it had never been organized in all those battles before Solferino.

The wounded from Solferino, and the other battles of the campaign, were moved to the city of Milan before being sent home. To avoid the worst of the heat, their removal took place at night. Dunant watched them being loaded into the trains. The spectacle wrung his heart.

"Trains packed with wounded soldiers entered stations which were crowded with silent, sorrowful people lit by the pale glimmer of pine torches. The crowd, a compact mass, all quivering with emotion and kindliness, seemed almost to stop breathing as

"If he came across someone he knew, he would kneel at his side trying to bring him back to life, press his hand, staunch the bleeding, or bind the broken limb with a handkerchief. But there was no water to be had for the poor sufferer. How many silent tears were shed that miserable night when all false pride, all human decency even, were forgotten!"

Henry Dunant,
from A Memory of Solferino

they heard the stifled groans which came from the carriages as they passed."

At Milan, far away from the battle, the wounded had been received as heroes. Even before Solferino, the Milanese hospitals had been crammed with nine thousand patients from previous engagements. Now, each night — night after night — one thousand more arrived by train. Every family who had a carriage sent it to the station to collect the wounded men.

Dunant had seen for himself what the words "Victory at Solferino" really meant. He was determined that other people should know — and would see to it that this sort of shambles never occurred again. "Shambles" is the right word — it is the old word for a slaughterhouse.

It was like a medieval vision of hell. Henry Dunant could not get out of his mind those cries of agony and fear: "Don't let me die!" "Water, for God's sake." He could not forget the men who had grasped his hands as they died.

In one way, you might say he was one of the casualties of Solferino. He had to have a little time to himself. He had to have some quiet time in which he could order his thoughts. He went up to the mountains to find peace.

The Paris years

Dunant's life was shattered. He had to begin again. His mind turned to the business interests that he had neglected in the great urgency of the battle. He set out for Paris, where he hoped to meet influential people and get the financial backing that he still needed.

Even though Dunant was a man charmed by elegant society and by rank and title, during the next three years his mind was still obsessed by Solferino. These bland, courteous men and women, complacent and preoccupied with their own concerns, began to exasperate him. He longed to break through their indifference. He wanted to force them to help him do something about those wounded in war.

Two years went by in Paris and then another in Geneva. His conversation became more and more concerned with his experiences. Eventually his listeners, bored and uneasy, turned away.

The chilling reality of war. Thousands of soldiers were hurriedly buried in the hills around Solferino. For years afterward local people brought the unidentified bones to this chapel so that the unknown soldiers could be given a decent burial.

In January 1860, he received the first of the awards for his work at Solferino — the Order of Saint Maurice and Saint Lazarus of Italy — but he could not shake off his depression.

When he went back to Geneva, the peace and beauty of his home seemed less real than the battle-fields of Italy. He began to believe that the only way he could live with them was to force himself to write everything down.

A Memory of Solferino

As he wrote, the confused ideas that had come to him as he cared for the wounded began to take shape. It seemed to him that he had been called by God to right these terrible wrongs.

"In this state of pent-up emotion which filled my heart, I was aware of an intuition, vague and yet profound, that my work was an instrument of His Will; it seemed to me that I had to accomplish it as a sacred

Driving through the fields and vineyards of the Lombardy countryside today, it is hard to imagine the agony of the Battle of Solferino, when the streams ran with blood and it took days to collect the wounded and weeks to bury all the dead.

duty and that it was destined to have fruits of infinite consequence for mankind."

Dunant had lived with his memories for a long time. Now that he put them down on paper his horror and his passionate concern came alive on the pages.

He wrote a book, *A Memory of Solferino*. Clearly and without hiding any of the facts, he described the slaughter, the efforts of the doctors, the courage of the soldiers — and the hard work and infinite kindness of all those, rich and poor, who had helped ease the suffering of these soldiers.

He did not stop there. He showed that much of the misery could very easily have been prevented. The conclusions he had come to as he watched the horror unfold were irrefutable. It seemed lunacy to leave preparations to cope with a disaster until the disaster actually occurred. Suddenly it seemed incredible that no one had organized help for those wounded in battle.

Other people besides Dunant had seen a need, but never with his blinding perception. Never with his ability to write so clearly. Never at the right moment.

A book to change the world

In *A Memory of Solferino*, he asked the vital question: "Would it not be possible, in a time of peace and quiet, to form relief societies of zealous, devoted and thoroughly qualified volunteers to bring aid to the wounded in time of war?"

Dunant argued that "a host of active, zealous and valiant helpers" could so easily have lessened the agony of Solferino. What had been required were strong, trained workers to scour the battlefield, to find the injured before they had been weakened by hunger, thirst, and exposure. Trained helpers could have guarded against living men being thrown into mass graves. Intelligently designed ambulances would have saved the wounded from intolerable suffering.

Letters could have reached the wounded, accurate records kept of the wounded and the dead, and the next of kin informed. There could have been official interpreters. Equipment could have been at the right place at the right time. Someone could even have planned to supply food and water to the wounded!

"In a few terrifying realistic pages all the horrors of mass slaughter were exposed. The impact on philanthropic circles was electric. It shook the whole of Europe."

Adolphe Pictet, literary scholar

And the work would not have depended on the emotion of the moment — a euphoria that could so quickly evaporate, leaving the wounded men helpless.

It was a new vision — and it was put before the world at exactly the right moment.

In September 1862, Dunant paid for the first printing of *A Memory of Solferino*. The reaction was electric. The success of the book astonished Dunant — it was overwhelming. Every copy was read and then passed from hand to hand until thousands upon

Dunant at the peak of his success, when he mixed with leaders all over Europe. He was determined to get support for his humanitarian ideas at the highest level. He used all his considerable energy and persuasive powers to win their important backing.

Gustave Moynier

Dr Louis Appia

Dr Th. Maunoir

thousands of people had read it. A second edition was put out in December.

Dunant had a great gift; he could speak and write in a way that made people feel personally involved. *A Memory of Solferino* was a flame that lit a great fire of enthusiasm and effort. It was a flame that led to the founding of the Red Cross.

The most important people of his time wrote to Dunant, acclaiming his achievement: the French novelist, Victor Hugo; the builder of the Suez Canal, Ferdinand de Lesseps; admirals, field marshals, administrators, and politicians.

Florence Nightingale sent a message too. She was impressed by the book, but she had reservations. She made one very sound point — and one that was to affect the development of the Red Cross. Dunant, understandably, was obsessed with the idea of aid in wartime. Florence Nightingale said it was vital that a system be established that would be equally effective in both war and peace. And she felt it would work only if done on a national scale.

General Trochu, who had been at Solferino, wrote to ask Dunant to look even further: "You have made no mention of evils more criminal still, inflicted on the innocent inhabitants who happen to live where the battle is fought…harvests destroyed, villages taken, retaken, set on fire, violence of every variety and of extreme brutality.…"

The monarchs of Europe were lavish in their praise.

The dream becomes reality

Dunant's ideas had excited people throughout Europe. But now came the long, grinding work of turning the vision into a practical, workable system.

An old acquaintance, a lawyer named Gustave Moynier, a man with little imagination but a most precise mind, came to see Dunant. He felt he could help turn the dream into reality. By their very natures, they did not get along too well, but they were to make a formidable team.

Moynier, the President of the Welfare Society of Geneva, worked with Dunant to draw up the outline of a new organization, an organization with individual national societies that would cooperate when necessary and that would recruit volunteer workers in time of peace.

The ideas of *A Memory of Solferino*, conceived in white-hot emotion, were to be given the reality of cold, hard fact. It had to be, though Dunant feared the effect such methods would have on his God-given vision.

Moynier did not have Dunant's fire, but he inspired the Welfare Society of Geneva to look beyond the confines of Geneva and consider a work of international importance.

The Society met on February 9, 1863, much as usual. But on the agenda was an item that was to change the world. It was the proposal as set out in *A Memory of Solferino* for the formation of permanent relief societies for aid to men wounded in action.

One of the people present at the meeting was Dr. Louis Appia. He had done a great deal of work developing a more satisfactory stretcher and at Solferino had made careful and professional notes of all that he saw. He was what they needed — an internationally recognized surgeon for the war wounded.

Henry Dunant

The Committee of Five

Four members of the Welfare Society were chosen to help Dunant put his ideas into action. They included Dr. Appia, Gustave Moynier, and Dr. Theodore Maunoir, a surgeon who would be of great practical help. General Dufour, a humane and respected soldier — and one of Switzerland's greatest men — brought acceptance and prestige to Dunant's ideas. All these men had proved their concern for the underprivileged. All were leading, respected citizens of Geneva. Together with Dunant they were known as the Committee of Five. Moynier, the legal mind, looked forward to international conferences where all the details could be thrashed out.

Dunant was rather unnerved by their cold-blooded efficiency — and spoke of the need to attract well-known people. He was proud of the great names who had congratulated him and given him support, and he felt he could call upon them to help the work. In nineteenth-century Europe, royal support gave a great

Gen. G. H. Dufour.

The men of the Committee of Five: Dunant provided the energy and enthusiasm to influence Europe's leaders. The others provided the prestige and practical backing that would turn Dunant's dream into reality. All four were leaders in their fields. They had worked for the suffering before and were highly respected in Geneva society.

boost to any enterprise. So Dunant sought it out.

Both Dunant and Dr. Maunoir were determined that from the very beginning the movement should have an international scope.

In the minutes of that historic meeting on February 9 were the words that seem to be the very root of the Red Cross. It was noted not only that volunteer nurses were to be sent to battlefields, but that transportation, hospitals, and treatment should be improved. The committee would have to be permanent and truly international in its concern. The sending of supplies would be helped, it was hoped, by the waiving of customs duties.

Finally, Henry Dunant insisted that the world powers agree to protect the safety of every official or unofficial relief worker coming to the aid of persons wounded in battle. This guarantee of safety would be written in the form of an international treaty among the various major governments.

It was at this time that Dunant learned that medical workers were shot if they went onto the battlefield to

The Europe shown on the map is considerably different from the map we know today. Solferino and other battles in Henry Dunant's lifetime were largely territorial. The red line shows Dunant's journeys across Europe.

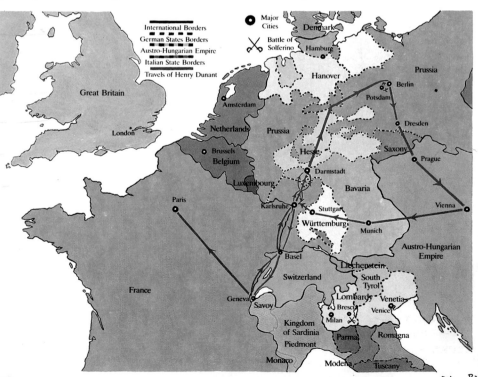

collect the wounded. This was because they would be dressed in military uniform. Like others before him, Henry Dunant wondered how this could be prevented. He would be the first person to find the answer.

To have its ideas put into practice, the committee needed a more official forum — so Dunant and his colleagues took the ambitious step of inviting specialists from different countries to meet in Geneva the following October. That conference was to become the birth of the Red Cross.

The European journey

Before the vital Geneva meeting, Dunant set off for Europe. He hoped that he could draw more people to his cause. He went from one country to another, pleading his case. His enthusiasm was infectious and his button-holing technique gained the new movement a good many converts.

In his enthusiasm he got carried away and, without consulting the rest of the Five, he sent out a circular stating his committee's aims.

It recommended that each government in Europe should give its protection and support to its own national committee to be organized in each capital city, with a membership of the most respected citizens.

Dunant argued that in time of war governments should allow medical and other supplies for medical workers to be sent to the war area. They should also send donations that their societies collected to help those who were wounded in war.

His circular also recommended that the governments should accept all military medical workers and their assistants, including volunteers, as neutral and therefore not participants in the fighting.

He was the first person to suggest that medical workers should not wear the army's uniform. This would prevent their being shot at. Instead, they should wear an emblem to show that they were not taking part in the fighting. It was a simple but brilliant idea.

Without the agreement of his committee, Dunant was putting forward the most important of his proposals — that of neutrality. He pushed the idea that certain people or groups can be on neither side in time of war. This idea was to be the key to all work done by the Red Cross from that day to this.

Dunant gained the support of some of the most important leaders in Europe, and several promised to send official representatives to the Geneva meeting. The journey was an outstanding success. Only Dunant could have achieved the support that was promised.

The birth of the Red Cross

On October 26, all was ready for the meeting. Even Dunant was stunned by the number of people who attended. There were eighteen delegates representing fourteen governments.

Discussion was laced with criticism as well as enthusiasm. One particularly odd delegate was a man named Twining from England. He felt the best solution was to humanely kill the very seriously wounded, after they had had time to pray "so that they should not die with a fevered brain and blasphemy on their lips." This was a methodical answer to the problem but one that, mercifully, did not get any support.

Dunant seeks more support

Dunant was very worried during the following year. His business affairs were in a chaotic state and he knew he should give time to them.

But he also instinctively knew how important it was to keep inspiring people to support the principles that had been agreed upon at the Geneva meeting. In a strange way, the Committee of Five, for all the differences in style, was ideally balanced. Dunant's dreams were backed by the practical help of the other four. And they could never have persuaded heads of countries to help and cooperate as Dunant could.

Now Dunant turned his attention to the United States — probably to the dismay of his more restrained colleagues. He had been delighted by President Lincoln's Declaration of Emancipation for the slaves in the United States in 1863. Now he begged for Lincoln's support at the conference. Although Lincoln sympathized, for political reasons he could not move. Two "observers" were appointed, however, and this encouraged Dunant greatly.

But Dunant's colleagues seemed to resent him and to be irritated by his enthusiasm. Things continued to go badly with his business. His spirits were at a low ebb. He wrote to Moynier, offering to retire from the committee. He felt of no further use: "It is now for those better equipped than I am, to promote its aims and to see that they are truly effective."

Moynier wisely wrote to tell him that he was still vital to the cause. After all, Dunant was the figurehead of the movement, the name that everyone knew and respected. He was also the only one on the committee capable of inspiring international support in the forthcoming conference.

The Geneva Convention

On August 8, 1864, the delegates assembled for the Diplomatic Conference. Sixteen nations had accepted invitations and had sent twenty-four delegates. It was a unique occasion — powerful countries of the world coming together to agree on a permanent set of rules for the treatment of those wounded in warfare.

On August 22, after a good deal of persuasion, eleven nations signed the ten articles that formed the first Geneva Convention.

This document — a milestone in the history of humankind — guaranteed neutrality for ambulances, hospitals, and medical workers and their equipment; for local inhabitants who were helping the wounded; and for wounded enemy soldiers. It also required their captors to treat their wounds or to arrange for this to be done. It spelled out the obligation of armies to search for and to collect the wounded. Finally, it established the red cross on a white background as an internationally known symbol of protection and neutral assistance in times of war.

All that was needed was formal approval by the governments concerned. By the end of the year, ten countries had done so, and by the end of 1867 the number had risen to twenty-two.

The signatures and wax seals on the First Geneva Convention, signed by eleven countries on August 22, 1864. This was a document that changed the world because it was lasting. It was the first multilateral treaty that didn't involve countries' ganging up to fight someone else. Instead the countries united in a time of peace to prevent suffering. The convention is the most widely adhered to of any international agreements. Since 1864 it has been continually updated by the International Committee of the Red Cross and has become much more wide-ranging and solid.

Problems in business

When the convention was over, Dunant left for Paris. He spent the next two years trying to improve his

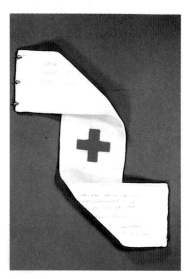

The new arm band, designed by Dunant and used for the first time in the Prussian-Danish war of 1864 by committee member Dr. Louis Appia. This simple symbol was, henceforth, to be a lifesaver for doctors, nurses, and all other medical helpers in times of war.

business. This had suffered drastically because of Dunant's neglect; his mind had been on his humanitarian work. Tragically, Dunant misread the signs — he did not recognize just how serious his business problems had become.

After a journey to Algeria, where he tried to gain land concessions, he returned to Europe only to find another war brewing.

On June 14, 1866, war was declared between Austria and Prussia. Dunant's dream had become reality, for the Prussians, who had signed the Geneva Convention, formed a relief society and planned carefully how they would deal with their wounded. The Prussians lost fewer than ten thousand men. But the Austrians, who had not acted, suffered twenty-five thousand casualties.

The Austrian wounded lay hidden in woods and ravines, suffering just as the men of Solferino had. Some were not found for two days. In one area some volunteers discovered three hundred men lying among eight hundred of their comrades who had died of neglect and exposure. There were no dressings, no bandages, no blankets. Gangrene took its toll as it had in 1859 — for the Austrians things had not changed.

The victors wrote of heroism and patriotism and God-given victory. Dunant read the statistics and shuddered in horror.

At the end of the war, a great celebration was staged in Prussia. Dunant was a distinguished guest. He shared in the praise and the glory and was carried away by the music, the glittering uniforms, and the banners, including that of the Red Cross.

Later, Dunant met the Prussian king, who told him: "At the time you came to Berlin in 1863, I was the first prince in Europe to appreciate your work and give you encouragement. I had no thought at that time that we should so soon need the services of the organization you had founded. Our enemies, however, have forced war upon us. Today, all the nations have signed the Geneva Convention. Austria's was the last signature. Peace was made in August, and on the following day she gave her acceptance to the Convention. She was late with her undertaking. Her wounded were left to us," said the king. "We have given them all the care and attention we could: they had better treatment than our own wounded."

Dunant was overcome by these words. It seemed almost impossible that his own ideas, half-formed at Solferino, had already saved thousands of lives.

Ruin!

But despite the growing success of the Red Cross, personal disaster struck Henry Dunant. In 1867, at the height of his international success, his business went bankrupt. All of Dunant's money was taken to pay the debts — as well as his home, his properties in Switzerland and in other countries, and a large part of his family's fortune.

Although other directors of his business seem to have been equally to blame, Dunant was not there himself to answer his accusers, so he was held principally responsible.

In 1868, the Court of Civil Law held him publicly to blame for the disaster. He was held to have deceived his colleagues, and this verdict was published in the Geneva newspapers for all to see. The initial loss of money was due to his preoccupation with the Red Cross. But was the final mishandling of his business deliberate deception or simply lack of attention to detail and bad management? We will never know.

At the age of forty, just nine years after Solferino, Dunant had lost everything. He had lost his standing as a citizen of Geneva. He was bankrupt, branded as the cause of the disaster publicly and, worst of all, he lost his position in the Red Cross in Geneva.

Dunant went bankrupt for almost a million Swiss francs — a huge sum in those days. Bankruptcy in Geneva at that time was always a total disgrace. But worse still, family and influential friends felt personally betrayed and angry. Many would never forgive him. Henry Dunant vowed to himself that he would work to repay the debt and clear his name. But this disaster ruined his life. He would not even recover his prestige for nearly thirty years.

Humiliated, Dunant left Geneva forever.

"Surely, if those who make the slaughter can claim a place on the roll of honor, those who cure, and cure often at the risk of their lives, are entitled to their due of esteem and gratitude."

Henry Dunant,
from A Memory of Solferino

31

The beginning of the bleak years

Living in simple lodgings in Paris, Dunant suffered deeply. He had valued his family name, his respected position, his well-to-do and influential friends — and he was away from home without his family's support. The future looked hopeless.

In the summer of 1867, Napoleon III staged the *Exposition Universelle* in Paris, and the Red Cross took the opportunity to put on a display of equipment, with a laurel-crowned bust of its founder in the middle. Dunant, humiliated beyond belief by the contrast between his fame and his disgraced condition, got someone to quietly remove it. The bust of the arms manufacturer, Alfred Krupp, which stood nearby, was left to hold the limelight.

Krupp received the Grand Prix for the Krupp gun. Dunant, Moynier, and Dufour received gold medals for services to humanity. No one seemed to notice the contrast in the choice of these awards.

However, Dunant was growing a little more hopeful, and he started to plan a way to clear his debts. Every award also helped to cheer him a little more. He was made an honorary committee member of several countries' Red Cross societies and was praised at national meetings of the organization.

In July he was summoned into the presence of Napoleon III's wife, Empress Eugénie. She was distraught, for she had just heard that in a naval battle off Italy over a thousand men had died through lack of neutral aid. She felt it was vital that Dunant do something about it. Sadly, he told her he now had very little say in such matters, but she ignored his protests. He was the man who could and *must* do it.

He promised to do what he could, but he knew he had little influence now in the Red Cross. Too many Swiss people had followed their hero and lost money because of him.

Henry Dunant was living on a shoestring budget. His mother sent him encouraging letters and a fur coat to fight off the terrible cold of the Paris winter. But

The principle of neutrality for medical ambulances had now been accepted by armies — but no such protection applied at sea. In July 1866, at the battle of Lissa, a thousand soldiers died on just one ship, the Re d'Italia, *because no neutral hospital ships were available. Dunant fought hard to extend neutrality to sea battles. This goal was achieved at the Second Geneva Convention in 1899.*

soon she died — a great blow for such a devoted son — and on top of this his hopes of a recovery in business faded again. At every opportunity he spoke of the achievements of the Red Cross and its future aim and succeeded in winning many to its cause. He was disgraced in Geneva, but Paris and the rest of Europe still saw him as the leader of the Red Cross movement.

He succeeded in getting the question of neutrality at sea onto the agenda of the first International Red Cross meeting in Paris that August. Empress Eugénie strongly promoted what she felt to be her personal cause. She spoke persuasively and strongly for the importance of rescuing sailors and hammered home the idea that hospital ships should be organized, and protected, in the same way as land-based hospitals.

The subject got as far as being made a draft clause to be added to the 1864 convention, but failed to get the backing that was necessary for its adoption. The proposal was not finally to be adopted until the Hague Convention of 1899.

Dunant busied himself with a scheme to set up an international library and another to provide a homeland for Jews in Palestine and to set up projects there. Both schemes were impractical and generally underfunded, but Dunant tried very hard to get them started. He continued to feel deeply concerned about slavery and to work for the improvement of prison conditions. Many of his ideas were years ahead of their time. But most of his dreams would one day become reality.

By 1870, the firepower of armies was reaching a grim efficiency, with guns that could fire shells 1,600 yards (1,460 m). Henry Dunant watched with growing horror as such weapons were developed. With his usual prophetic vision, he warned that before long, humanity would have used science to acquire such phenomenal means of destruction that nothing short of divine intervention would be able to save the world from total destruction.

War again

In 1870 France declared war on Prussia. The casualties on both sides were terrible — over 100 thousand killed. The Prussian wounded, as a direct result of the Red Cross, were speedily removed to well-organized hospitals. But the French wounded did no better than at Solferino, eleven years before. Finally, on September 2, at Sedan, the armies clashed in a decisive battle. France's Napoleon III surrendered rather than let any more people die.

Above: Within two years of the signing of the Geneva Convention, the Red Cross was highly organized in several countries. It was prepared to take responsibility for evacuating and treating the war wounded.
Right: The inside of a specially designed hospital train. At Solferino and all previous battles, the wounded had been transported in ordinary carts or railroad cars. By 1871 equipped ambulances and medical trains were already in use.

A Dutch ambulance team during the Franco-Prussian War. Across Europe, Red Cross relief societies were designing equipment and training volunteers during peacetime in preparation for giving humanitarian aid during war. When the Franco-Prussian War of 1870-71 broke out, non-involved countries, including Britain and the Netherlands, were able to send well-equipped volunteers to help.

The siege of Paris

As a new French government was formed in Paris, the city came under siege by Prussian forces. Dunant, along with the rest of the population, was trapped.

Once again he found himself in the thick of someone's war. And once again he devoted himself totally to helping the wounded. He was not alone. Small Red Cross groups were active across Paris, and Dunant's ideas were working in a situation of almost total chaos and panic.

The Red Cross symbol was recognized by all. An Englishman carrying half a million francs to assist the French wounded went through the lines under the Red Cross flag. He was amazed to find the symbol saluted by those he passed, whether civilian or soldier.

For four months, Paris was under siege. Bombs fell and the Parisians were forced to eat horses, rats, cats, and dogs. By December it had grown bitterly cold. Dunant worked tirelessly, collecting warm clothes and bandages to distribute to the needy.

In January 1871 the armistice was signed and French officials turned to Dunant for help. They asked him to try to save two supporters who had been

Below: Paris starved during the siege in 1870. Many people used the newly designed hot-air balloon to escape.

captured by the Germans. The men had been wounded and were due to be shot — when they had recovered. Dunant set off for Versailles and the Prussian High Command. He was stopped over and over again for questioning. On his arrival, he was arrested and taken off to see the Chief of Staff. Once again, the old magic of his power to state a case succeeded, and to his joy the men were released.

Civil war — the Commune

The devastation caused during the civil war and siege of Paris in 1870 was horrible. Some major buildings were reduced to rubble by repeated shelling. Combat was savage. Across the city, Red Cross groups battled to provide medical help and food for the starving. Dunant, again a noncombatant, worked tirelessly to organize help.

The Germans had gone. Paris was free. But the misery was not over. Feelings flared and on March 18, 1871, the revolutionary Commune took power.

Dunant bravely went to the Commune's headquarters to request observance of the Geneva Convention: "I treated them as gentlemen and they addressed me as a citizen of importance." They assured him that the Red Cross would be respected.

The uneasy peace was broken when a trigger-happy sentry shot a surgeon. The surgeon had been unwise, for he had walked freely in the street showing no Red Cross, the sign of his neutrality.

In revenge, ten thousand government soldiers attacked, and the Parisian prisoners they took were shot immediately. Paris, on learning this, went mad with fury. From now on there was to be open war, with little justice or mercy. Men who carried a white flag were shot down, and priests were arrested.

Dunant kept his head in the chaos that followed. He tried desperately to reach people he believed to be sane and reasonable and begged them to see that the wounded and captured would be protected. To Dunant's horror, they refused to listen. All was revenge and reprisal — death to the enemy.

This man, who seemed in ordinary times so insignificant and confused, continued to act with astounding courage. A priest had been captured — a good and harmless man who had been working to save the children of Paris. He had gone on wearing his clerical clothes — and that was enough for the mob. They wanted him dead. Dunant faced them and got the poor man released into his care.

Mob rule

Dunant's worst fears were realized. By May 24, Paris was burning. The executions on both sides were as indiscriminate and cold-blooded as at the height of the French Revolution. Fear pervaded the city: men were killing-mad and people were shot for any reason or for none. Priests, police, innocent civilians were rounded up and executed.

On Sunday, May 28, after seven days of terror known as the "week of hell," the last barricade fell to the invading forces. The French leaders commanded that Commune prisoners be treated with mercy. But they were slaughtered by the thousands. Dunant was numb with horror. What could even the Red Cross do against such bestiality?

After the Commune

With the war over, the authorities set to work restoring the country to some kind of normality. But no one who has lived through such hell can ever be quite the same — certainly not Dunant. Having experienced Solferino he had never expected to live through such horrors again, but in some ways this civil conflict seemed to have been even worse.

The bankruptcy, the disgrace, the loss of his home, wealth, and friends had marked Dunant for life. The barbarism of the siege of Paris and the atrocities of the Commune were yet another disaster for him.

He was now forty-three; for a few more years he battled on. He still worked for great causes. He managed to lecture on peace and putting an end to slavery. He worked for prisoners and prisoners of war. But he was a shadow of his former self.

Dunant and some of his friends formed a World Alliance for Order and Civilization, also called the Universal Alliance of Order and Civilization. In some respects, it resembled the United Nations today. The group was convinced that it was not enough to patch up the damage done by war — people should strive to prevent it. Again, this visionary man was working for a concept that would only happen decades later.

In Paris, Dunant had seen prisoners of war suffering. If they were no longer simply killed outright, not

The mob burned, looted, and killed. The slaughter during the Paris Commune was as bad as that at the height of the French Revolution. Dunant showed great personal courage in facing the mob. On one occasion, he stood before a firing squad to save a man's life.

enough care was taken of them. As in earlier battles, all this was accepted as normal.

Dunant was determined to change matters. The Red Cross had already begun to act for prisoners of war, even though they were not covered by the Geneva Convention. Dunant wanted to push things further. So he drew up his own charter. It had five requests.

One was that "the prisoner should be provided with all that was strictly necessary for his well-being; he should have facilities for communication with his family and friends; his journeys to camp or for repatriation should have an accepted standard of comfort; the prisoner who died should have a decent burial and a record made for his relatives; good feelings should be prompted between the prisoner and the people against whom he had fought."

The question was discussed at the Congress of the Universal Alliance in June 1872, but though a committee was set up, Dunant was no longer well enough, or wealthy enough, to travel Europe as he had in the past, putting his case to the influential authorities. Partial protection of prisoners of war did not come about until the Hague Conference of 1907. Mercifully, Dunant lived to see that. But he did not live to see the Geneva Convention of 1929 that finally saw the adoption of the ideas he had fought for, over fifty years before.

Forgotten

Nothing Dunant tried seemed to prosper. His ideas were still as visionary as before and many of them were to succeed in the coming years. But they were to succeed without him.

For eleven years he lived in poverty. He moved from Paris to London, back to Paris, to Stuttgart, to the Isle of Wight, to Trieste, to Corfu, and back again to various German cities.

He was permanently ill, suffering from a painful skin infection called eczema, especially in his writing hand. From the occasional reports of him, he seemed to have become suspicious, irritable, and quarrelsome. He never had enough money and his existence can only be described as miserable. Most people in

Europe would have presumed that he had died. He was certainly forgotten.

This time spent outside society had left Dunant not only ill, but terribly depressed. The years after Solferino had seemed so full of energy and hope. Now he looked back on half a lifetime of disappointment and poverty. Dunant longed for a little dignity once more and a little self-respect. Long years of hunger, shabbiness, loneliness, and lack of a useful job were driving him into self-pity and bitterness.

His only consolation was seeing the Red Cross becoming more and more accepted. The growth was phenomenal. Already Dunant's ideas had saved thousands and thousands of lives.

Country after country had their own Red Cross groups who spent the years of peace preparing to help the war wounded. Bandages were rolled, volunteers were trained, ambulances were designed.

There were several territorial wars in the late nineteenth century as countries united to become the European nations we know today. The fluttering Red Cross flag became a familiar sight in war. Bands of trained nurses, stretchers, linen, and every medical item that might be needed followed each army. The ordinary soldier would not be forgotten now.

In 1876 Turkey adopted the Red Crescent symbol instead of the Red Cross. The Red Crescent would spread to Muslim countries across the world. By 1888, thirty-four countries already belonged to the Red Cross or the Red Crescent.

Above all, the clauses of the Geneva Convention were holding firm. The world's first international treaty was becoming permanent. Country after country was signing. Thanks to Moynier and the Red Cross men in Geneva, the humanitarian idea was growing.

Well-off German ladies prepare dressings and blankets during the Franco-Prussian War. In these early days, Dunant's exciting ideas aroused a great deal of enthusiasm. The strength of the Red Cross back in Geneva was that it was already directing this charitable zeal into highly efficient expertise that would make it possible for the Red Cross to work over the entire world.

Heiden — home to Switzerland

In July 1887, at the age of fifty-nine, Dunant made the journey to Heiden, in eastern Switzerland. Here was the beauty and peace of his childhood. Dunant quietly but proudly told people that he was the founder of the Red Cross, the promoter of the ideals that became reality at the Geneva Convention. He needed people to know — he needed to feel that he was more than a sick, shabby, and forgotten man.

Heiden, he learned, was also what he needed. For so long, everyone he had had contact with had been involved in his causes. Even the wounded and the prisoners had become statistics. Now, once again, he was with ordinary people who made no demands, who had no influence — but who were glad to let him be at peace. Dunant the idealist slowly became Dunant the man. To his astonishment, children liked him. He found great pleasure in being with them.

During the five years he lived among the villagers of Heiden, he became far happier, but the long years of struggle and disappointment had scarred him. He felt he had been wronged. He was touchy and liable to take offense, even when people were trying to be helpful. But he continued to write about inhumanity and his beliefs about what should be done.

Dunant's hand grew far worse, so his doctor felt that he should be moved to the hospital. He was to have a little bedroom and a study overlooking the lake.

In 1892, at the age of sixty-four, he moved into the hospital with his few possessions and, after a little fussing, settled in. He was to live there for the last eighteen years of his life.

Fame and recognition

Dunant lived in Heiden in almost total obscurity. He wrote letters to old contacts, trying to get recognition for his life's work. He received polite replies, but he was out of the limelight. He would probably have remained so until the end of his life if a young journalist had not been climbing in the mountains nearby in 1895. In casual talk, the journalist had picked up stories of an old man — the founder of the Red Cross — living in the hospital at Heiden. Like any reporter, he recognized a good story and wrote to Dunant asking for an interview.

Dunant, seeing a chance to promote his ideas again, was glad to see him and Georg Baumberger, the journalist, had enough sense to treat the old man with great respect. Dunant had grown suspicious, but the young man was genuinely interested. Encouraged,

Dunant began to tell the story of his incredible life.

Baumberger was excited. Here was everything to make a superb article — kings, battles, negotiations, plans, suffering, courage. Dunant thrust press cuttings and manuscripts on him. It was as if he wanted to tell the truth through this young man.

It was over thirty years since the publication of *A Memory of Solferino*, but the public had remembered. The article brought an overwhelming response. Dunant could scarcely believe the letters that flooded into Heiden. Friends came, old acquaintances. Money came too — and Dunant, who was long used to the fear of destitution, put it all into a bank, against any future "rainy days."

He was staggered. It appeared that years before, Napoleon himself had offered to pay half of Dunant's debts if his friends would cover the rest. But everything had gone wrong. The letter that could have given Dunant a second chance was missing. Later, some of his admirers suspected that it was no accident. Too many influential people had wanted Dunant silenced and forgotten.

Homage now came from Red Cross and Red Crescent societies throughout the world. Dunant's whole life seemed transformed. Suddenly he had recognition — and money too. Pensions, awards, and prizes overwhelmed him.

He seemed to come back to life under this rain of refreshing compliments. He began to write again and he began new projects.

He wrote one last impassioned appeal for peace. All the wonders of modern invention were being used for war — and the creators of new methods of bestial destruction were admired. Borne up by a new euphoria, he implored the nations of the world to take notice of his message: "There must be disarmament in the heart: there must be brotherly love."

Several of his early ideas were now coming to fruition. The Hague Convention in 1899 had extended the Geneva Convention to sea warfare, and the treatment of prisoners of war was being regulated. These two decisions meant more to him than any award.

Then, in 1901, came the ultimate international acknowledgement of Henry Dunant's achievements.

One of the two simple rooms in Heiden Hospital where Dunant spent the last years of his life. He continued to write passionately about his dreams for peace. He had led an extraordinary life. Until the age of thirty-one, he had devoted himself to the service of the poor. Then came the dramatic turning point of Solferino, followed by devastation, then fame and success, then bankruptcy. He then survived fifteen years of rejection and poverty and fifteen further years of fame during which he never left these rooms in Heiden, Switzerland.

1988: A stamp celebrating
the 125th anniversary of
the Red Cross.

*Dunant had led a
wretched existence in his
wanderings, sometimes
sleeping on street benches
and in railroad waiting
rooms, his body craving
food whenever he passed a
bakery. Now, at last, he
found peace.*

The Nobel Committee decided that the first Nobel Peace Prize should be shared by Dunant and Frédéric Passy, a man Dunant held in great respect. It brought Dunant prestige. It brought prestige to Switzerland. It helped heal his feelings of deep humiliation.

The last years

During the last years of his life Dunant read a great deal, and in his reading he discovered new tales of suffering — not of soldiers or prisoners, but of ordinary men and women caught up in the changing world of the industrial revolution. He saw poverty and evil working conditions and the exploitation of children. He held them in his mind — but he was past fighting for them. He was not to know about the work the Red Cross and Red Crescent were to do among such people in the years after he was dead.

Dunant made his will — as honest and fair a will as one would have expected from such a man. The money from the Nobel Prize had not been touched. He asked that once all legal claims had been satisfied, anything left over should be shared by various charities. He also established a place for homeless people at the hospital in Heiden.

He died on Sunday, October 30, 1910. He was eighty-two years old.

From the strange, muddled man of Geneva, whose vision was almost too much for him to bear, came a movement that today stretches to every corner of the world. It has reached millions of people. It brings help to soldier and civilian alike, a reality even greater than Dunant's dream.

"There is no man who more deserves this honor, for it was you, forty years ago, who set on foot the international organization for the relief of the wounded on the battlefield. Without you, the Red Cross, the supreme humanitarian achievement of the nineteenth century, would probably never have been undertaken."
International Committee of the Red Cross, 1901,
on the occasion of granting the first Nobel Prize for Peace

This diagram shows the signatories to the Geneva Convention (the left-hand branch) and the year-by-year founding of Red Cross societies (the right-hand branch) up to 1913, shortly after Henry Dunant's death.

In memory of Henry Dunant

Henry Dunant died in 1910. By that time, fifty-seven nations of the world had signed the Geneva Conventions, and forty-three countries had formed their own national Red Cross or Red Crescent Societies.

Now, 125 years after the founding of the Red Cross, 165 nations have signed the Conventions, and there are 146 national Red Cross societies. No other treaty in the history of the world has so many signatories, and there is no other humanitarian organization with so many members in so many countries. In the pages that follow we review the extent of the work now undertaken by the Red Cross, from providing first aid cover at a protest march to handling thousands of tons of supplies for famine victims. There could be no finer tribute to Henry Dunant than the modern Red Cross in action around the world.

Above: A massive consignment of food parcels moving into Germany in the closing months of World War II.

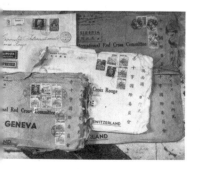

In World War II, millions of letters passed through the Red Cross to POWs.

Dunant's legacy

When Henry Dunant died in 1910, at peace with the world at last, he could hardly have imagined the growth that was to take place in the movement he had done so much to promote. Half a century had passed since his fateful journey to Solferino, and in that time the Red Cross had spread to more than forty countries.

Now the International Red Cross and Red Crescent Movement is the largest humanitarian organization in the world, made up of people of different races, beliefs, and political convictions. They are all united for a common cause.

Red Cross and Red Crescent workers are active in peace and war, bringing help and reassurance. Four years after Dunant's death came World War I. The horror far outstripped that of Solferino — but by now there were trained volunteers to take care of the

wounded, with ambulances and field hospitals ready to come to the aid of these wounded men.

People called it "the war to end all war" — and when it was over, the Red Cross turned its attention to relieving suffering brought about by other causes — famine, epidemics, and earthquakes. The League of Red Cross and Red Crescent Societies was formed in 1919 to get people involved in relieving this suffering and to coordinate these peacetime activities.

But war refused to go away: the next major conflict was World War II. Newsreels brought the slaughter of the front line into the homes of ordinary people. Prisoners of war were herded into camps all over the world. The Red Cross again did what it could for the victims, as it has done in the conflicts that have continued to ravage the world since 1945, in Indochina, Africa, Central America, and the Middle East.

Left: Wounded prisoners from the Iran-Iraq war being repatriated as laid down in the Geneva Conventions.

Right and below: POWs must be treated well and allowed to communicate with their families; the ICRC's visits help to protect those rights. When civil strife breaks out in a country, people are sometimes arrested for security reasons. The ICRC asks to visit these detainees, to see that they are treated well.

The treatment of prisoners

The Geneva Conventions, agreed upon by almost all the countries of the world, say that prisoners of war must be treated decently: they must not be killed or tortured; they have the right to shelter, food, clothing, and medical care; they must receive the letters and parcels from their families; and their camps can be inspected by a neutral agency such as the International Committee of the Red Cross (ICRC), the body that Dunant helped to found.

During his lifetime, Dunant fought to have some kind of legal protection extended to prisoners of war. But it was not until 1929, nineteen years after Dunant's death, that prisoners of war were protected under the Geneva Convention.

When two countries are at war, they must allow the ICRC into the prison camps. These days, though, many of the prisoners that the ICRC visits are political detainees, people who are not protected by the Geneva Conventions. In these cases the ICRC has to negotiate with the authorities before its staff can enter the prisons. For this it relies on its reputation for strict neutrality—not taking sides. This is helped by the fact that the ICRC delegates are all from Switzerland, a neutral country.

A fleet of Red Cross buses moves women and children to safety out of a besieged town in Lebanon. For months the area had been encircled by hostile forces and cut off from the rest of the country; the Red Cross was the only lifeline for relief supplies. Getting agreement for the evacuation took weeks of negotiations.

Protecting civilian populations

In World War II, civilians were affected by the fighting as never before: the bombing of cities, the reprisals against villagers, deportations, and mass extermination. In rules introduced since then, starting with the Geneva Conventions of 1949, the world community has laid down standards for protecting civilians.

But civilians remain at risk, often cut off from food supplies and medical care, forced to flee their homes to escape the fighting. Many Red Cross emergency operations today are aimed at protecting and assisting civilians by providing essential supplies and, above all, by being present in the conflict zones. In these tense situations, Red Cross and Red Crescent workers always have to be firm in ensuring that relief goes to those who really need it.

47

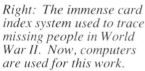

Right: The immense card index system used to trace missing people in World War II. Now, computers are used for this work.

Below: "Have you seen my son?" Families who are trying to trace missing loved ones turn to the Red Cross.

Tracing missing people

One of the most heartbreaking situations that occurs in a war is not knowing what has happened to a daughter, a brother, a mother, a father. In the bombing, the chaos of battle, the forced marches, did they survive or didn't they? Where are they now?

Since 1870, the Red Cross has strived to find the answers. Its Central Tracing Agency, based in Geneva, tries to keep families in touch. In World War I, for example, the agency opened files on seven million missing people and was at times handling thirty thousand letters a day from anxious families.

In World War II, over 100 million letters were exchanged, through the agency, between prisoners of war and their families. For civilians, the problem was equally vast: millions of people had been uprooted from their homes. Many of them had been sent to labor camps in other countries; others had simply vanished. At the end of the war, the Tracing Agency helped to reunite 700 thousand people with their families. About twenty-five percent of the agency's work today still concerns cases from World War II.

An essential factor in the agency's success is information: names, addresses, and other vital facts found in lists, letters, anything that might identify someone. These details, regarded as strictly confidential by the agency, are carefully stored so that one day they might be matched with a request for information from a relative or friend.

Over forty years apart: Natalia and Galina Golovacheva, two sisters from the Soviet Union, were deported to Germany in 1942. Before the war had ended, Galina escaped to Belgium; Natalia returned to the USSR. After making some unsuccessful inquiries, each sister came to believe that the other had died. Then Natalia had a last try: her request for news went first to the Red Cross in Moscow, then to the Central Tracing Agency in Geneva. The Agency's files revealed that Galina and her husband, an ex-POW, were in Belgium — so then the Belgian Red Cross took up the search. She was found and finally reunited with Natalia at Moscow airport in a tearful but happy meeting.

An ongoing task

Since 1945, the Central Tracing Agency has been involved in practically every conflict; its files contain over sixty million cards. Each year it transmits more than two million Red Cross message forms among members of separated families and reunites or repatriates about ten thousand people affected by conflict.

The Tracing Agency often works closely with the tracing services of the national Red Cross and Red Crescent societies — for example, in the case of the Vietnamese boat people: all around Southeast Asia, a network operated to register these refugees and try to put them back in touch with their families.

"During World War II, a list of prisoners was written on a cigarette packet and thrown off a train. Someone found it and sent it to us."
Tracing Agency official

Above: Kampuchean refugees in Thailand perform a drama to show the brutal treatment prisoners can suffer at the hands of their captors if the principles of the Geneva Conventions are not followed.

Below: Children in war-torn Ethiopia reading books supplied by the Red Cross. Because of the fighting in their country, their basic understanding of Red Cross principles could save lives.

Getting the message across

As Henry Dunant proved in his lifetime, in conflict the basic ideas of the Red Cross and the Geneva Conventions need to be understood by everyone — soldiers, rebels, governments, and ordinary civilians. People's lives depend on it.

Having rules to lessen suffering in war is no good unless people know about them. This is why Red Cross and Red Crescent workers the world over are spending more and more time trying to get the message across, through meetings, books, comics, plays — and even by putting themselves between violence and the victims. Recently in South Africa, a community worker shielded a wounded man from the mob in the doorway of her Red Cross office.

The laws of war

Apart from the worldwide movement he left behind, Dunant's greatest legacy was the protection of war victims, as set out in the Geneva Conventions. The first convention covered soldiers on the battlefield. Later this was extended to protect sailors.

In all this, the International Committee of the Red

An ICRC worker prepares to show a film to government troops in El Salvador. In any situation of civil strife, the code of humanitarian conduct must be explained to all who do the fighting — whatever side they're on.

Below: "Respect civilians" — a vital rule when men, women, and children find themselves in the front line.

Cross has played an important part, as it did in Dunant's time, in getting governments to agree to these measures.

The last major revision of the conventions took place in 1949, when governments and the public alike were still scarred by the events of World War II. But with the different kinds of conflicts that arose during the decolonization period, especially guerilla warfare, new rules were needed; these were introduced in additional sections, known as Protocols, in 1977.

While all these laws are very detailed, their basic message is plain: people who do not take part in the fighting (civilians) and those who no longer take part (prisoners and the wounded) must be protected from harm and treated humanely.

51

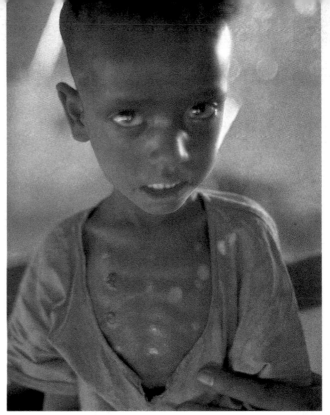

When civilians are threatened with starvation, food supplies must be rushed in — often in vast amounts. Development projects are needed to defeat some of the causes of famine.

Opposite page: Endless lines of people waiting for a food distribution in Chad. Hunger can be brought about by natural causes or by war; in both cases, help is needed immediately, and even after the immediate emergency is over.

Feeding the starving

In many parts of the world, families do not get enough to eat — not just for one or two days, but all the time. Children suffer the most from the lack of food or from having the wrong kind of food, because their growing bodies need regular, healthful nourishment. Without it, it is harder for them to fight off disease. In the most extreme cases, very little stands between these people and death. So when the situation suddenly gets worse — because of war or some natural cause such as crop failure — they can quickly become ill and die. Ethiopia, Sudan, and Mozambique are just some of the places where this has happened.

The Red Cross, like other charities, responds to these emergencies by sending food and other relief. But it also sets up programs to help people grow enough food for themselves, plant trees, and dig wells to try to keep famine at bay. These are jobs for the national Red Cross and Red Crescent societies and their federation, the League.

A worldwide network

Whenever a major disaster strikes anywhere in the world, an appeal for help is received by telex in the Geneva headquarters of the League of Red Cross and Red Crescent Societies.

Since it was set up in 1919, the league has coordinated over one thousand international relief operations to help the victims of earthquakes, cyclones, volcanic eruptions, floods, and famine.

As the federation of 146 national Red Cross and Red Crescent societies, the league operates a worldwide network of assistance. It makes sure that relief supplies are sent to the disaster area fast and without duplication — ordering blankets from one country, medicines from another, a transport plane from another, and so on.

The league's staff and field delegates — doctors, nurses, transport specialists, administrators — are also truly international, coming from many of the countries represented in the movement. Apart from relief operations, an important part of their job is to help build up strong Red Cross and Red Crescent societies everywhere, with good preparation for disasters as well as health and youth projects.

The league also assists in the care of refugees outside areas of conflict — in Southeast Asia, Pakistan, Africa, and Latin America. And it represents the national societies in the international field, working with the United Nations and other relief and development agencies.

Survivors of the horrible mud slide in Colombia in 1985. Since 1919, the League has helped the victims of more than a thousand major disasters.

Preparing for disaster

The sheer scale of Red Cross work can sometimes be hard to imagine. When an earthquake happens, or fighting breaks out, thousands of people become homeless. They have to be fed and cared for and quickly.

The first people involved are the volunteers of the Red Cross or Red Crescent society of the country where the disaster has happened. With so many people to serve, their stocks of food and medicine can soon run out. They then contact the league in Geneva, which maintains its own warehouses around the world, and thousands of tons of supplies can be shipped to the disaster area.

In most countries, the Red Cross spends a lot of time training its volunteers in the principles of first aid and preparation for disasters. And in Bangladesh, a country hit by cyclones and floods every year, the league and Red Crescent are building vast shelters on stilts in which whole villages can find safety until the storm is over.

When the Red Cross swings into action, it presents a picture of humanity at its most caring. Tons of food, medicines, trucks, and ambulances, which have been paid for by ordinary members of the public from around the world appear as if from nowhere, to help those in need. Henry Dunant, if he were alive today, would be amazed and delighted by the scale of it all.

Two Chinese children learn first aid skills. The Red Cross societies throughout the world encourage young people to learn first aid, because this is one way everyone can be ready to help.

Training in first aid and welfare

One of Henry Dunant's dreams was that everywhere in the world there would be a body of trained volunteers ready to help others in times of war and peace.

Today, all national societies offer their members training in first aid so they can cope if they are on the scene of an accident or if a major disaster happens, if people are hurt in the mountains or on the beach or, more likely, when someone collapses in the home or on the street.

Research by the American Red Cross shows that more people in the United States know how to start their cars with jumper cables than to give the "kiss of life." Thousands of lives would be saved yearly if everyone learned basic first aid. Young people can help society without waiting to become adults. Special youth training is offered in most countries.

Many Red Cross and Red Crescent societies also offer welfare services — for old people, hospital patients, drug abusers and, increasingly these days, for AIDS sufferers.

Aiding people with disabilities

After the Battle of Solferino, Dunant saw many soldiers who had lost arms and legs in the fighting. Soldiers continue to be mutilated on the battlefield. Civilians continue to be paralyzed or blinded by bombs. Children continue to wander into minefields and have their legs blown off.

Since its founding, the Red Cross has been concerned with the disabled. Today, the ICRC maintains special hospitals for victims on the border between Afghanistan and Pakistan, in Africa, and elsewhere. Training victims in new skills so they can earn their own living can go on for a very long time. After the 1985 earthquake in Mexico City, the league provided many people with artificial limbs.

At the national level, the Red Cross and Red Crescent organize special programs for people with mental or physical handicaps. The Dutch Red Cross has a special boat, the Henry Dunant, *to provide vacations for these people. Such projects give young Red Cross workers the chance to help others.*

Above left: Entertainment at a special medical center set up in Angola, in southern Africa. It was set up to help all those who lost limbs in the civil war there. Providing artificial limbs is an important part of the work after many wars and natural disasters.

Above right: The Swiss Red Cross does a great deal to help people with disabilities. It has coaches adapted for wheelchair users and each year takes over twelve thousand people on trips to the countryside. The ICRC and the league, also based in Switzerland, have other such projects.

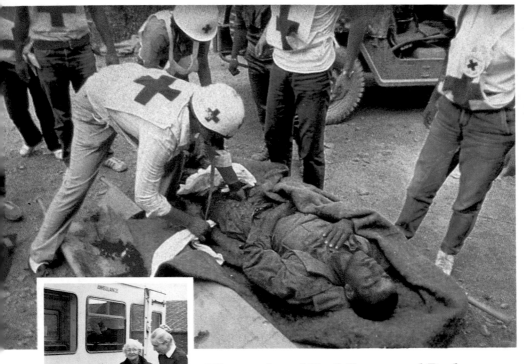

The national Red Cross and Red Crescent societies

Today there are recognized Red Cross and Red Crescent societies in 146 countries, with others being formed in about fifteen more. Henry Dunant's dream of a universal movement covering the whole world is now very close. The Red Cross symbol is used by 122 countries, and twenty-three Muslim countries use the Red Crescent, while the Soviet Union uses both. But each symbol has exactly the same protective value in international law.

The movement now has around 250 million members, of whom about half are young people under the age of twenty-five. All members are pledged to support the movement's fundamental principles of humanity, impartiality, neutrality, independence, voluntary service, unity, and universality. These guarantee that the Red Cross and Red Crescent societies work only to prevent and ease suffering, without any discrimination and without taking sides in any conflict. The goal is clear: these societies are designated to

Above: The basic training of these Lebanese Red Cross workers saved many lives when Beirut was hit by fighting in the 1970s and 1980s.

Inset: A Red Cross volunteer helps an elderly person. Much of the work in times of peace is unspectacular but just as humanitarian as the work done in time of war.

58

Providing wells for villages, like this one in Nepal, is a common feature of Red Cross and Red Crescent work in the Third World.

promote mutual understanding and lasting peace among all the peoples of the world.

However, in such a vast movement there are bound to be differences of emphasis at the local level. All national societies provide first aid training. All recruit blood donors and, in some countries, run the blood transfusion service. All have youth sections, letting young people help others in a practical way. But other services are provided according to local needs: training nurses in Mongolia, disaster workers in Michigan, and relief staff in Mozambique; digging wells in Ethiopia; helping earthquake victims in Ecuador; running international youth camps in Egypt; planting trees in Mauritania; caring for refugees in Malawi; staffing first aid posts in the factories of Moscow....As one slogan puts it, the Red Cross and Red Crescent is "Everywhere for Everyone."

From its beginnings on the battlefield of Solferino, the movement has grown into the world's largest humanitarian organization. Its members are still motivated by Henry Dunant's vision.

Hope for the future — the essence of all Red Cross work — is personified by this young Ethiopian volunteer. Her plants will help fight off the desert.

Portraits of Nobel Laureates in Peace. Wintterle and Cramer (Abelard)
The World's Refugees: A Test of Humanity. Loescher and Loescher (Harcourt Brace Jovanovich)

Magazines

These magazines will give you more information about events related to health and relationships among the various peoples and nations of the world. Check your library or bookstore to see if they have these magazines, or write to the addresses listed below to get information about subscribing.

Current Health 1
General Learning Corp.
P.O. Box 3060
Northbrook, IL 60065

Faces
P.O. Box 6991
Syracuse, NY 13217

Junior Scholastic and *Scienceland*:
In the United States:
P.O. Box 644
Lyndhurst, NJ 07071-9985

In Canada:
Scholastic-TAB Publications, Ltd.
Richmond Hill, ON L4C 3G5

Glossary

Adversary
An opponent or an enemy; someone who opposes someone else.

Allied
United by an agreement. One country, person, or group may join with another one or more to be stronger than a single country, person, or group would be.

Alms
Money or help for poor people.

Barricade
A defensive structure, usually built quickly during street fighting from whatever may be handy, such as carts, bed frames, or barrels. Barricades were a particular feature of French politics during the nineteenth century as a way for ordinary people to attract attention to a problem that would otherwise have been ignored.

Bayonet
A long, knife-like blade that fits on the end of a rifle.

Charter
A written contract or grant providing a person's rights or a settlement with a government; or a document, such as a constitution, that formally outlines the principles, functions, and structure of a corporation or some other organization.

Colonization
Settling in a new location but continuing to be governed by the home country, or country of origin.

Commune, Paris
The revolutionary government that ruled Paris from March 18 to May 28, 1871.

Comrade
A friend, or someone who shares something in common, like activities, interests, or philosophies.

Concession
Something that one person allows another person to have, especially as a way toward settling a disagreement.

Convention
A formal international agreement.

Crescent
The shape of the moon in its first or last quarter, when it is less than half. The Red Crescent groups use this symbol instead of a red cross.

Cuirassiers
Cavalrymen wearing close-fitting armor made of leather.

Dragoon
An armed soldier who can fight on foot or on a horse.

Eczema
A skin disease that causes the skin to become scaly in patches and sometimes to ooze a clear liquid. These patches itch and burn almost unbearably. Nowadays it can be controlled with drugs, but Dunant could only have put a soothing lotion on the patches. This gave little relief.

Emancipation
Freedom from slavery or bondage.

Empire
The complete rule of a large area by one or very few people.

First Aid
The immediate medical care given after an accident or emergency. It can be as minor as putting on a plastic bandage or as major as mouth-to-mouth resuscitation and heart massage. The national societies of the Red Cross and Red Crescent train millions of people in first-aid techniques every year.

French Revolution

The uprising against the king and the church in France that went on between 1789 and 1799, when Napoleon I seized power. During this period thousands of people were executed by the guillotine, and much land changed hands.

Gangrene

The decay of body tissue and parts due to lack of blood circulation.

Geneva Conventions

International treaties that lay down rules which are valid in conflict to protect people who do not take part in the fighting (civilians) or who no longer take part (the wounded and sick, prisoners of war). The Geneva Convention of 1864 protected the wounded and sick on the battlefield. It was later extended to include victims of war at sea (1899) and prisoners of war (1929).

In 1949 a major revision took place, resulting in four conventions that covered the wounded and sick on land and sea, prisoners of war, and civilians in enemy-controlled territories. In 1977 the conventions were updated and amended to take into account developments in modern warfare. Out of 171 nations in the world, 165 are now party to the conventions.

Hague Conventions

A series of conventions adopted at conferences in 1899 and 1907, with the aim of regulating methods of warfare. They include rules on the treatment of prisoners of war, restrictions on permitted means of waging war, the prohibition of dumdum bullets (bullets with small noses that expand on contact, causing huge wounds), as well as rules on the bombing of cities.

Lancers

Soldiers who are armed with lances, which are spear-like weapons.

Monarchs

Kings and queens, who inherit their positions of power.

Musketry

Groups of soldiers armed with muskets or other small guns.

Neutrality

In international relations, the position of a country that does not take sides in a disagreement between or among nations.

Outcasts

People who are rejected by society.

Partisans

Civilian soldiers who fight against enemy forces that occupy their country. These people must sometimes work underground because they fear for their lives and the lives of family members and friends if they criticize occupying forces in public.

Patronage
Granting favors to friends and supporters from a position of power, usually political or financial power.

Rations
A specific amount of food and supplies. In times of war, food is often rationed, or given out, in small, tightly controlled quantities.

Repatriation
Returning to one's country of birth or original citizenship. People who have left their home countries during a war are often repatriated after the war.

Saber
A heavy sword with a curved blade, used by cavalry.

Shrapnel
Metal pieces from an exploding artillery shell.

Chronology

1828   **May 8** — Jean Henry Dunant born in Geneva, Switzerland.

1847   Dunant visits poor people and prisoners in Geneva's prisons.

1849   Dunant is apprenticed to a banking house in Geneva.

1853   Dunant helps form the World Union of Young Men's Christian Associations (YMCA) in Europe.
With his appointment as general manager of a subsidiary bank in Algeria, Dunant makes his first business trip to Algeria.

1855   First YMCA World Conference held in Paris.

1858   Dunant turns his Algerian business into a company.
He publishes *Notice sur la Regence de Tunis*, in which he attacks slavery.

1859   **June 24** — Battle of Solferino is fought between France, Sardinia, and Austria in northern Italy. Witnessed by Dunant, it leads to his writing *A Memory of Solferino*.
June 25-27 — Dunant works nonstop day and night aiding the wounded in Castiglione.

1860   Dunant receives the Order of St. Maurice and St. Lazarus of Italy for his work with the wounded after Solferino.
His Algerian business is doing badly.

1862   Dunant publishes *A Memory of Solferino*. In it, he suggests forming an international relief society of volunteers to care for the wounded in wartime.

1863 **February** — The Public Welfare Society of Geneva sets up a Committee of Five to back Dunant's ideas.

Dunant is a driving force in organizing the International Committee of the Red Cross (ICRC).

October 26 — The birth of the Red Cross. A conference of eighteen representatives from fourteen countries meets in Geneva and recommends the formation of national relief agencies. The red cross symbol is adopted to identify helpers on the battlefield. Dunant is thirty-five.

1864 **August** — The first Geneva Convention. Diplomats from sixteen European states gather to form the Diplomatic Conference in Geneva. They sign "The Geneva Convention for the Amelioration of the Condition of the Wounded in Armies in the Field." It was a convention concerning the humane treatment of all sick and wounded soldiers and the protection of medical staff and other people who are not taking part in the fighting.

1867 Dunant's business fails and he leaves Geneva forever.

The Netherlands Society calls itself "The Red Cross Society of the Netherlands." This is the first society of its kind to identify itself as the Red Cross.

1870 The ICRC begins forwarding lists of prisoners so that their families will know what has happened to them. This practice leads to the creation of the International Prisoners of War Agency in 1914.

1870-71 The Franco-Prussian War and the Siege of Paris. Dunant organizes food, blankets, and entertainment for the troops.

This war results in atrocities on all sides. Dunant helps victims of the revolutionary government, the Commune of Paris, escape. He also tries to intercede with the German and French military leaders who are besieging the Commune. Dunant is forty-three years old.

Dunant begins sixteen years of obscurity (until 1887), living as far afield as London, Corfu, and Stuttgart, doing various low-paying jobs. During these years, he continues to work against slavery and to help prisoners of war. He also campaigns for the Geneva Convention to be extended to naval warfare.

1875 The Geneva Committee adopts the title of the "International Committee of the Red Cross."

1876 The Turkish government adopts the red crescent as its symbol of neutrality. Other Muslim countries follow suit.

1887 **June** — Dunant settles in Heiden, Switzerland. He is fifty-nine and ill.

1892 **August** — Dunant moves into the local hospital in Heiden, which becomes his home.

1895 Dunant is interviewed by Georg Baumberger, whose article about him gains Dunant wide recognition.

1899 The International Peace Conference is held at The Hague. The Second Geneva Convention extends protection to the wounded and shipwrecked as a result of naval warfare.

1901 Dunant is awarded the first Nobel Peace Prize with Frédéric Passy, who founded the International League of Peace.

1906 The First Geneva Convention is revised and updated.

1907 The Second International Peace Conference is held at The Hague. The resulting Hague Convention extends protection to prisoners of war.

1910 **October 30** — Dunant dies in the hospital in Heiden at age eighty-two.

1914 The International Committee of the Red Cross extends its efforts to natural disasters as well as wars.

1919 **May** — The League of Red Cross and Red Crescent Societies is founded in Paris by American Henry Davison. Its goal is to help the Red Cross societies across the world "in a systematic attempt to anticipate, diminish and relieve the misery produced by disaster and calamity." By 1920, twenty-three national societies start an ambitious international program.

1920 The Junior Red Cross Bureau is opened.

1928 The International Red Cross — now a truly unified international relief agency — is founded.

1929 The Third Geneva Convention lays down rules for the protection and care of prisoners of war.

1949 The first three Geneva Conventions are updated and a fourth is added to protect civilians detained in enemy countries or occupied territories.

1960 The Prisoners of War Agency becomes the Central Tracing Agency. Its goals include tracing people missing because of conflict, reuniting separated families, and sending messages between prisoners and their families.

1977 More new provisions are added to the Geneva Conventions.

1988 Volunteers numbering 250 million in 146 national societies around the world belong to the Red Cross. It is the world's largest humanitarian federation. It helps develop the national societies, coordinate relief operations, and care for refugees outside areas of conflict.

Index